An Eclipse and a Butcher

Ann-Chadwell Humphries

An Eclipse and a Butcher

Ann-Chadwell Humphries

Edited by

Ed Madden

The Laureate Series

AN ECLIPSE AND A BUTCHER.
Copyright 2020 by Ann-Chadwell Humphries.
All rights reserved.

Printed in the United States of America. No parts of this book may be reproduced in any manner without written permission except in the case of brief quotations embodied in critical articles and reviews.

Library of Congress Control Number:2020947172
ISBN:978-1-942081-27-2

Cover Art by Susan Craig and Eleanor Baker

An Eclipse and a Butcher by Ann-Chadwell Humphries is the second book in the Laureate Series, an endeavor by Muddy Ford Press to celebrate the tradition of poetry that is born to South Carolinians, and to promote and honor the relationship between Mentor and Protégé,
Advocate and Postulant,
Poet and Poet.

The Laureate Series

The Laureate Series

Dedicated to my parents, Charles and Barbara Chadwell; my siblings Cindy, Mary, Chad, and John; and my husband and partner, Kirk.

Contents

Introduction 3

I

A Portrait in Bronze of the Eclipse 7
Baptism 8
Three Dreams 9
A Doe In Repose 10
Nine Horses 11
Hurricane Matthew 12
Swimming the Frio, Circa 1965 13
Cliff Swallows at the Wateree River 15
The Kite Boy from Bangladesh 16
The Bench 17
The Virtual Tour 18

II

My Father's Birth 21
Catch-light 22
Four Songs 23
Nine Days 25
Three Histories 27
Tuna Salad Sandwiches 29

An Eclipse and A Butcher 31
The Escape 33
My Mother's End-of-Life Directives 34
Three Portraits 35
Say the Words 36
There Was a Stone 37

III

Fine with Blind, A Self Portrait 41
Say Yes 43
Summer of '77 44
Balance of Power 45
Listerine 46
Winter Orange 47
A Friendship Blessing 49
Touch Tour of Rare Books 50
An Artist Renders the 1918 Eclipse 51
The Washout 52
To Think I Almost Missed These Paintings 53
Noble Cause 55
A Gift To Myself 57
Portrait of a Husband 58
Fallen Pine 59

Epilogue 61
Acknowledgements 63

Introduction

Three eclipses punctuate this book.

The first is the most recent, and Ann Humphries reminds us that whatever we thought we knew, something about the experience could surprise us, the book thus opening with what "we had not expected." And whatever we wanted to know or learn, the experience was gone before we could grasp it. It may be "A Portrait in Bronze of the Eclipse," but bronze is not solid, it is the evanescent metallic light that limns the scene for a moment, then disappears. It is a moment of perception that is gone before we can capture what it was, what it meant.

The second eclipse is one from her childhood, a memory—like many poems in this book—about family and growing up. But memory here is neither sentimental nor nostalgic. She is aware that unspoken relations stitch every scene, determine how we move through the world and what it offers us. In this poem, we see small local lives lit and dimmed by histories both personal and public. Over and over Humphries offers little stories in which family, geography, catastrophe, nation are gravities that may push us together or pull us apart. What happens far away—in time or space—casts a shadow on what is near.

In last eclipse of the book, in 1918, an artist tries to capture that fleeting perception of the eclipse, tries to capture in paint what photographs fail to record. To see differently is to see more accurately.

In all of these, of course, we are mindful of warnings not to look too close or too long—staring at the sun can make you blind. Threaded through the book are poems about coming to terms with blindness. Humphries insists that she is "Fine with blind" late in the book, but over and over she demonstrates that that vision is more than what we see—that we may know who we are and where we are by touch and sound, by friendship and family, and by memory, the distant sun that lights this book.

This is a book of resilience and beauty—and love, there is so much love in this book. There are poems of bracing directness and delicate description. I love the economy of her language, how a portrait can be sketched in one line, how straightforward language can carry unspoken cargoes of meaning, how the loss of something is not darkness but a moment that may limn the world around us with its rippling, unexpected light.

Ed Madden
Poet Laureate
Columbia, South Carolina

I

A Portrait in Bronze of the Eclipse

We had not expected metallic light
bunched as we were in solar glasses.
Opened our arms to it, beseeching,

as if to catch the color like drops
of rain or hold a robin with both hands.
But the light would not be contained. It cast

shadows crisp as pencil lines. Ripples
skittered over our shoes and across
the sand. The air softened

like night when clouds rouged the
horizon. Then it was gone.

Baptism

His family straight as stalks,
fix their eyes on him as sunflowers follow sun.

Dressed in white: short pants, long socks,
he peeks over the pleated shoulder
of a black robe, cants his eyes
from parents to pastor
who dampens his hair three times—
Father   Son   Holy Ghost.

After the service, I step into
the light of his mother's smile,
pat his back.

He reaches for me
curls a dimpled arm
around my neck
presses the petal of his ear
to my cheek, and it is I
who am anointed.

Three Dreams

In 1960s Kodachrome
three sisters less than three years apart
sit cross-legged, un-self conscious
hair tousled, streaked with sun,

playclothes rumpled across their chests.
One squints, elbows on knees. Another
shades her face. A third straight-backed,
blue eyes wide with surprise.

Three sisters tossed in the air by their father
scamper to a bubbled bath and crowd the tub.
One by one hoisted by their mother
toweled dry, hair fragrant with soap.

Three girls giggle into gowns
before supper and stories.
Sisters tucked in one bed loose-limbed,
shallow breaths curl from each other to dream,

dreams that one day will pull them apart.

A Doe in Repose
~Beldoc, South Carolina

A fresh kill, she looks peaceful
diagonal across the northbound lane.
Here, black asphalt whips through
tree farms, burnt corn, picked cotton.
The 35 mile-per-hour limit
holds vigil for her as she lies
before the abandoned cafe.
She must have been flushed from safety

by last night's storm. Should we stop?
We ease beside—
deer ticks rim her eyes.
The next morning, blood smears on bent grass.
Turkey vultures feast on her carcass.
Someone kinder— braver—
dragged her to the ditch.

Nine Horses

Nine horses crowd a ranch house porch.
Dozens of hooves scramble for purchase
on the slick, sloped floor. Rumps buck

    as they stagger and shove
        against the rail.
Three horses mount the steps

eyes pelted with rain,
    hindquarters wrapped in whitecaps
from the river Conquistadors christened

    Brazos for arms of God.
helicopters whip waves into froth,
bank east to survey

roofs scattered like books
left page down on muddy plains.
To the west, desperate cowboys wave hats at hundreds
of steers streaming like grain

across Hwy. 290 to higher ground.
The storm drowns sounds of
cruisers' pinwheeling blue lights.

Six o'clock news pauses
on islands of stranded cattle

    trapped against fences
        they can't jump.

Hurricane Matthew

The latest forecast predicted
wind and rain on Sunday—
if they hurried, they could make
the noon game and drive back
that same day. The neighbor boy
would check on their dogs twice.
The storm turned inland, enraged
drowned the dogs in their crates.

Swimming the Frio, Circa 1965

Under the floating dock, the sun slants
its white curtain through green water.
In dime-store goggles, we pantomime
underwater conversation.

*

In a flash, we set a knife-blade stance,
coil with palms pressed and elbows cocked,
then lunge upward, slicing the water,
sweeping arms in wide circles,
racing bubbles to the top.

The muffled sounds we hear while we rise
crack against the surface,
becoming sharp and clear
as we thrust into the sparkling light.

*

On the dock, water slips from our bodies,
angled by collarbones, ribcage, and vertebrae.
We shake our heads, wiggle fingers in ears,

wrap towels around our waists,
tucked in knee-length sarongs
or toss them over shoulders,
poised to snap-pop bare limbs.

Slowed by a *No Running* sign,
we race stiff-legged down the ramp.
Our sandals flip as we hopscotch grassy patches
to the shaded picnic table

where watermelon waits.
We plunge into the lush sweetness.

Cliff Swallows at the Wateree River
~for you, travelers on the 601 Bridge

These chittering blue-backed bullets
stipple their sandcastle nests with

a thousand pellets of mud
—like oyster beds on concrete girders.
They lay their eggs, fledge their young

and in a month are gone.
And what of these fleeting moments?
Do you reverse course to attend?

It is for you.
                                      It is
                                                for you.

The Kite Boy from Bangladesh

Wind whips the half-buttoned shirts of boys
pulsing on sand cliffs that border the countries
of Myanmar and Bangladesh.
Dust kicks from their donated shoes, grit cradling
      in their baby teeth.
Gusts of sand sting their eyes—eyes with sight lines taut as string
to kites billowing in blistering heat.

Thin arms belie the authority
with which the boys commandeer their kites,
kites writhing like snakes, cocks
trailing glass-weighted tails, jesters
percussive with tassels and foil. Ancient rivalries
call these boys to manhood.

An astonished reporter asks, *Who makes these kites?*

Boys jab their elbows to Fayez,
a boy like them—stateless Rohingya
raw from ethnic cleansing. In his family's tent,
Fayez stitches plastic and fabric scavenged
on his routes for firewood. He splits
bamboo for frames. Ancestors guide
his calloused hands to test each kite:
fail, throws away; pass, gives away, gives away, gives away...

The Bench

D F Hernandez could gauge potential. Every
summer, he brought children from the west side
of San Antonio to camp in the Texas Hill Country.

On rounds with my father, the camp director,
he pointed to a common cedar stump:
That would make a nice bench. With chains,

the two men teased it like a tooth from its socket
of rocky soil. Opposite arms flew like fulcrums
as they quick-stepped it to the pick-up.

On three, they heaved it up and onto the bed.
The afternoon claimed them. They split the bench down
the middle, sanded splinters off the seat,

leveled it for children and dogs to jump. Light
enough to move about the yard, the bench
became a talisman— a focus for family photos,

a landmark for company. It moved with us
to South Carolina, strapped to the back of a U-Haul.
Last on, first off: Alpha and Omega. Soon after,

it was stolen. We could not track it, had to let it go.
Even in memory, the bench calls us to discern
value in roughness like D F Hernandez
saw in children from the west side of town.

The Virtual Tour

She counts-off nineteen steps to the porch,
crosses the threshold to plunge into a pool of April sun
planing through the picture window. She feels

its warm gold on her thighs. From the voices she knows
so well, she hears nuanced tones of their pleasure and pride.
They coach her to angle the lens to highlight

the red rocker, pie safe, son's self-portrait. The bound
    carpet leads
to the back door and courtyard with blue jays sassing in
    the sugar maple.
She weathervanes north south east west considers

where to hang a hammock. Back inside, she trails
    the chair rail
to the entry, curtsies her goodbyes, unfolds
a white cane to tap her way to the mailbox.

II

My Father's Birth

The couple found work at a corner bank
he met the public, she filed the papers,
took a loan on a car.

She worked until she showed
—company policy. When her time came
she was whisked to

the fourth floor, he
to the ground floor lounge in the
modern, antiseptic hospital unlike

the prairie where his mother was born. First baby,
her labor was long, muted by the twilight of
morphine and scopolamine.

Their baby arrived lusty and pink.
In her confinement, she dozed
to box fans stirring the July air

from the ward's open windows.
Ten days, then home. She changed
the baby day and night

for her husband to sleep. August turned
September, and by October
the baby slept through to morning until

the twenty-ninth when
the stock market crashed
and no one slept.

Catch-light

There are miracles in Columbia.

Beneath Gervais Street Bridge a pearl moon
tilts its pitcher to pour a Milky Way—
stars sequin the Congaree,
glisten granite and riverbank,
glint the eyes of God's urban creatures
bind with the catch-light of earthly dreams.

Four Songs

Hospital Elevators

Where are the elevators?
I think they are this way.
Look at her kick in the incubator!
How long must she stay?

One month, and then we celebrate—
She gets to go home today.
Where are the elevators?
I think they are this way.

Kathryn Banking

Act like you know what you're doing.
I'd like to deposit this check,
papers stamped, signed, triple cross-checked
at the drive-through, sweating, praying.

The teller squints, mathematic.
I'm sorry, you have to come in.
Act like you know what you're doing.
I'd like to deposit this check.

A Pair of Shoes

I am sending you a pair of shoes.
I wish I had shoes my mother wore,
shoes that don't fit me anymore.
We were so poor, she had to choose

to do without for me, too used
to the few pretty things she could afford.
I am sending you a pair of shoes
I wish I had shoes my mother wore

She gave me what I'll never lose—
I held her and held her before
she died. I wish I could hug her,
thank her, talk to her like we do.
I'm sending you a pair of shoes.

Home from the Hospital

The garage door shudders
car doors slam, and
footsteps stress the ramp—

she at the window.
They bump walkers to
press their foreheads for a time.

She circles his neck with her arms
and they dance again
to Xavier Cugat live.

Nine Days

I don't want to hear
the house was torn down—I wore
my wedding dress there.

*

On her way to work
past pink dogwoods, she saw a
horse on the sidewalk.

*

I stand on my head
in the corner—discipline
for new perspectives.

*

He unwrapped the cloth
to polish my glasses to
gleam in April's light.

*

The camera crew films
a reporter in the storm—
traffic signs fly by.

*

I move my sleeveless
dresses to the guest closet
and switch for sweaters.

*

I mark my keyboard
with dots, place my fingers there
and begin to type.

*

Corsage on her wrist,
she covered her smile to hide
the gaps in her teeth.

*

She snapped my portrait
in fall foliage—said, *There's
your funeral picture.*

Three Histories

Camp Sorghum, late 1864
~the ruins near Riverbanks Botanical Gardens

In an open field above Saluda rapids,
I guard fourteen hundred Union officers
who dig troughs by hand and cut limbs for shelter.
Unfit to fight, I was drafted for these last days.
Twenty men share one broken spoon for meals
of rationed cornmeal, mostly roughage and weevils.
Like them, I eat it raw with sour sorghum.
Can't remember when I was paid, so I take bribes.
Wearing rags this winter day, we march
to the walled asylum to wait for Sherman.

Columbia's Irish Canal Digger, circa 1820

We signed the manifest as indentured servants.
From County Cork, Kerry, and Clare
boarded ships bound for American prosperity
to carve canals past Congaree turbulence—
work for which slaves were too costly to spare.
We fought loneliness with fiddles and campfires
until claimed in death by fever and exposure.
I rest in a riverbank beneath a faded marker—
our legacy, a city of light and water.

Portrait of A Young Harriet Tubman, circa 1869

—the only one of her young, poised in an elegant
blouse ruched at the cuff and shoulder, pin-tucks
tapered to the waist, her forearm languid
on the back of a parlor chair, slender
fingered. In her lap, her left-hand casts
freighted shadows on her billowing skirt,
her eyes are wrought iron.

Tuna Salad Sandwiches

Almost done with her half day,
Yolanda asks if there's anything else she could do.
Abuelita, mater familia
reaches for her walker, asks,
Can you stay for lunch?

Do you have any tuna?

Both the woman and her husband perk up,
I think we do.

The trio pad to the farmer's table
where the husband pulls a chair for his wife
in the good light
that shines through the picture window.

A wife of sixty-three years
finds her glasses
shakes out the paper.

With measured steps, her husband
makes his way to the pantry
where he rummages for the tuna,
finds it and raises it like a prize.

Their kitchen is not one Yolanda has frequented.
Not asked to cook for them before,
she finds a knife neat in its drawer
and a bowl in its ceramic stack.

The two work in easy silence
He punctures the can, works his way around the rim,
holds the lid to drain in the sink.

Yolanda chops onion on the butcher block,
sweeps the glistening pieces onto her knife,
brushes them into the bowl
with boiled eggs and pickles.

The gentleman deals sliced bread
like playing cards,
selects the stemmed glasses his wife likes,
sets them before her
with cloth napkins and placemats.

Yolanda stacks the tray of fat sandwiches,
wipes clean the butcher block,
places the knife neat in its drawer,
the bowl in its stack,
gathers her things to leave,

Turns and sees three plates
and the man standing by a chair
he holds for her in the good light
shining through the picture window.

An Eclipse and a Butcher

Howard Brice had a soft spot for my mother.
He'd plug wedges in watermelons for
our family to taste. He'd drawl, *No good; no sale*.
Brice's Mercantile was one of only
two grocery stores in the county seat

(population 397) in that remote Texas Hill Country.
Saturdays, my mother, whom people said was
more beautiful than Jacqueline Kennedy,
piled the four of us into a '58 station wagon
—no seat belts nor air conditioning—

to drive thirteen miles past sheep and goats,
summer camps and tourist cabins
to the tiny market on the courthouse square.
When we pulled in, we kids tumbled out
to race through the screen door.

Not yet ten, I was entrusted to order our
usual three pounds of hamburger. When
I approached the lighted case, Mr. Brice
sang out, *How is Miss Ann today?* We talked
about the great white Pyrenees puppy

he had given us. Raw, red meat coiled
from his grinder. He swept a quivering pink pile
to weigh on a silver scale, wrapped it
in white paper, flourished the price with
a black wax pen, then slid the bulging
package gently to me. I thanked him
as I had been taught, found my mother
with our little brother in her overflowing buggy,
      then joined my sisters
at the candy counter. That Saturday

was July 20, 1963. At checkout,
we asked Mr. Brice for cardboard boxes
to make our pinhole projectors. On
our way out, we passed San Antonio
papers which headlined the President

and Mrs. Kennedy's pending trip
to Dallas. But on that day, in the gravel lot
of a small town's grocer, a family
turned its back to the sky
to watch
the moon slide across the sun.

The Escape

He's not been able to drive

Backs the car into the sun
reclines the seat for a nap
drives back in, bones warmed.

My Mother's End-of-Life Directives

My mother wants to outlast her teeth.
Said so for years
prefers to precede her descendants
as if declaring so would make it true.

Says she could bear
if anything were to happen
to me or my siblings—
you're middle-aged, you know.

But to lose the next generations,
our children or their children,
would devastate her as much as
my father's malignancies

the first when we were so young
the second when teenagers.

She sobbed to him after surgery
Why you? Why you!
Why not me? he whispered,
chest tube draining.

Lately, all she prays for
is a quick quiet death,

but if it's lengthy we'll deal with it.

Three Portraits

Olivia

Age five, hums as she plays

Corwin

All arms and legs, has an Olive Oyl frame

Whispered

Let's not have this conversation here

Say the Words
~instructions from my mother

When I die, Say the words
say that I died
say, She died
say, My mother died
not that I passed
passed away, passed on
nor that you lost me
I am not lost, I am dead
say the words
say that I died.

There Was a Stone
~after "In the Middle of the Road" by Carlos Drummond de Andrade

In the middle of my breast there was a stone
there was a stone in the middle of my breast
there was a stone
in the middle of my breast there was a stone
a history of false positives
tempted me to miss my mammogram
      had I missed
the mammogram would not have shown
high-grade ductal carcinoma
        never shall I forget
           there was a stone
              there was a stone
there was a stone in the middle of my breast.

III

Fine with Blind, A Self Portrait

I have made my peace. I am fine with blind.
Five senses become more, include my sense
of humor, an asset when forced to change
my life. I imagine how people look.
With iPhone technology, I can touch
a button and rely on my hearing.

The world opens to me by my hearing
spoken text online designed for the blind.
I stay current, connected, and in touch
with public conversation. This makes sense.
The transition has been hard, but I look
forward—not back—as I adapt to change.

Let's go out, he says. I clap, *Let me change.*
A booth in the back, please. We sip, hearing
jazz playing softly. He offers, *You look
beautiful.* We chat and laugh—love is blind.
Prized time with each other makes common sense.
We split dessert for the finishing touch.

To eat, I slide my fingers to touch
the place setting. To cut my food, I change
utensils with my hands, then switch.
My sense of surroundings begins upon hearing
daily specials. Folks can't tell I am blind.
During conversation, I turn to look.

On walks, friends warn of low, wet limbs, *Look
out!* Though I like to feel plants, I learned not to touch
cactus or poison ivy as a blind
hiker. Nature trips provide welcome change.
I hop river rocks, pausing mid-stream, hearing
birdsongs, waterfalls, and wildlife I sense.

With only light perception left, I sense
others' presence. Though I can't see, I look
toward your eyes. I find my way hearing
Follow my voice. I slide my toes to touch
the edge of stairs and make a level change.
I use tricks to work around being blind.

Blindness provides insight. My sense of touch
becomes my sight, and now, I welcome change.
With hearing and healing, I thrive as blind.

Say Yes

Would you like to feel the tree?
The live oak with weighted limbs.
I almost said *no, but thanks*,
But opened my cane to trace it.

Summer of '77

Iwas twenty-three with a CB
radio, traveler's checks,
and a fat stack of maps.

I was sure this would be
my only chance to be wild, to be free.
I spent seven weeks and my savings.

My ride: four-on-the-floor,
a sunroof, and wind in my hair.

Thought I was something. Drove.

Balance of Power

In our early days, he called me Partner
wrapped my wrist with a bracelet of Equal Rights
sprung the coil of my laugh
shook out wings of What Might Be.
We wed, shared a bed, children,
signatures on a mortgage.

When a recessive gene ravaged my eyes
and claimed the keys to my car
we adjusted to one driver, pressed
bump dots on the washer-dryer,
hung clothes by texture.
But poison habits creep like ivy.

I let him wave me from the kitchen
open my mail, sign my name
—we reasoned this was faster.
His voice grew dull, our banter flat
he hid in himself, out of my reach
What was this wilderness?

We had to name it.
When we pried open routines
ideas rushed in like happy dogs.
He agreed to afford me
the privilege of mess and mistake.
I agreed to save him

for what only he could do:
find gloves I lose when I hurry
whisper my hair looks a little wild
and at night, call me outside
to follow the beam of his arm
and find the full moon.

Listerine

My husband is a creature of habit
drives the same routes, shops the same stores
only buys Dentyne, Irish Spring.

We provision each day with gentle courtesy
—look for each other, kiss a shoulder bent to coffee.
      This morning,
I find him making my side of the bed

his back to me. I encircle his waist
lay my head on his back, feel him nod
—his mouth full of Listerine.

Always the original flavor with the ginger bite
same brand his family used
in the white wooden house where he was born.

He keeps a replacement under the sink
same size as the jumbo iced tea glasses
his mother filled for the men after church.

I hold to him while he props the pillows, smooths creases.
Finished, he faces me in his road race t-shirt
takes my hands in his and lifts them to his lips.

Winter Orange
~in memory of Sara Scruggs

From her breakfast table, she stares
out the south window. Bare branches reveal
her neighbor's deck—their forgotten mop

leans against a tilted bucket. Before her,
the pepper mill sits half full; salt crusts
on the shaker; paper napkins, prim in their basket.

She glances at her cookbook collection
noting her favorites, the frayed bindings taped
for another New Year. Another New Year?

The solstice sun slants further onto her gingham cloth
—first bright from the east, then high midday,
lengthening from the west. The shadows sweep

clockwise around wrought-iron candlesticks.
Absently, she smooths the pathology report.
Ink stains her fingertips. The words bounce wild

in her mind, hounds trail her fear as she crashes
through briars in territory unknown, desperate
for escape. But I, the winter orange, call to her.

I travel topographies and time zones
to rest in her fluted bowl. To her, I say,
Hold me with both hands. Behold my rich color.

When you pierce my skin, I anoint you.
Inhale. Let my fragrance calm you.
Let my shaggy threads weave hope in your heart.

Let my leathery core, pliant and strong, center you,
and my cool, sweet juice nourish you. Come to me.
Choose me. Accept my blessing.

After a time, she rises from her table,
reaches for her apron
and the rest of her life.

A Friendship Blessing

When others are gone, let us be your company.
When you feel restricted, let us restore you.
When you have places to go, let us take you.
When you can't see a way, let us make one.
When you are reluctant to ask, you can ask us.
When you offer yourself, we welcome you.
When you want to dance, we will be your partner.
When you want to sing, we will play the music.

Touch Tour of Rare Books
~for Elizabeth Sudduth

Seven stories to descend to the vault,
each floor as if passing a century,
In my hand, a medieval bible bought

at auction—text written 1240—
from the library's rare book collection.
Vines and flowers gild the cover, gold leaf

edges fragile pages fragrant with vellum.
I press clasps and hinges, reverent—
tactile permission on two conditions:

clean hands and pure heart.

An Artist Renders the 1918 Eclipse

Howard Russell Butler preferred oil and canvas
to the physics he studied at Princeton,
Earned fluency in the language of pigment
could name all the hues of blue.

He commanded a lexicon of motion—quiver, flare, drag
honed from the commissions for a dozen
portraits of Andrew Carnegie,
a restive subject for two-hour sittings.

That June, while the Great War raged,
Butler set his easel on a rural plain in Oregon
in the company of scientists and telescopes.
Cameras had proven inadequate. They wanted Butler.

Everyone readied themselves, Butler chose a blindfold
to dark-adapt his eyes. At the precise moment,
an astronomer signaled. Butler's graphite scored his paper,
The air moved from the brisk strokes of his sure hand.

After two minutes, the astronomer warned them.
Butler retreated to his impromptu studio on-site,
blocked out colors and movement on canvas
he saw with his eyes. From this, he created paintings

which a century later, still hold their force.

The Washout
~*Sesquicentennial State Park*

Twenty-one inches in twelve hours
shoved its weight through weakness.
A maniacal force gouged a cavity chest-deep

a quarter mile long. A raw wound left
to fester. I cannot stay away. It compels
me to make a weekly pilgrimage

to the altar of frayed yellow tape and
No Trespassing sign, unable to imagine
how this damage could ever be repaired.

Suddenly, a jogger lithe as a deer springs
from the woods, headphones like inverted antlers,
leaps over fallen trees, boxing low hanging branches.

I scissor my arms overhead, shout *Go back!*
Point to the warning flags, because
I know to pick my way through danger,

because I know its ugly power, because
I have nursed others through poor choices,
because this land is fragile, and I love it.

He eyes me—old enough to be his mother—
cuts his eyes to the crater, nods, and brushes by
as if I were a washout.

To Think I Almost Missed These Paintings
~for Will South, Curator, Columbia Museum of Art

I wavered to go, not probe the wound, the strife
of what I lack, the inaccessible brush
thick with paint. I request a tactile tour rendering
my right to be there. The curator motions
to a landscape which opens to us, my hand
flies with his, his gestures as wild as the painting,

Flower Beds in Holland, an early painting
finding its way. Mid-ground, a gardener strides
among beds of hyacinths, lifting rough hands
to his breast pocket for pipe tobacco. Brush
strokes throb with untamed emotion.
Flat-iron clouds roil across the rendering.

Will paints the air with his words, rendering
a crowd clicking their cameras at each painting.
Stretching our hands in sweeping motions
he frames the size of each canvas. Fat black swipes
fly as crows; green lines trim a goatee while brush
tips feather reflections with the surest of hands.

A woman whispers to her brood, *She's tracing
       Van Gogh's hand-
written Vincent* raised in bronze rendering
his signature tangible. Primal brush
marks dignify the subject of this painting
a peasant woman in profile, her face wiped
with age, her hair cropped in one coarse motion.

Linseed and oil scent frenzied motions
of desperation in the artist's hand,
his self-portrait evidence of a life of strife.
Bullets blaze from his blue eyes, rendering
us immobile in the presence of this painting,
our feet weighted where he wielded his brush

all his work as intimate as the brush
of a kiss resplendent with emotion.
To think I almost missed these paintings.
Will tucked my hand under his arm rendering
us as if old friends matching strides.

Noble Cause

That's what I need, a noble cause
now that the children stoke their own fires.
As for me, I have plowed fields and slopped hogs

for worthy causes, registered opinions
that vanish like dry ice on lawmaker tallies,
served as Sunday School teacher

bazaar co-chair, neighborhood
newsletter editor
packaged, stamped and mailed all that

to the next generation
corralled favorite family stories
lassoed photographs into albums

chopped in half household inventory
weighed and measured it into parcels
for sons and wives and auctioneers

staked a claim on a smaller home
rode herd on renovations, lay funeral plans
in church files, signed contracts

on property beneath the pastor's window
surrounded by flowers and friends
boxed up interviews, awards

and newspaper articles, apogees of career orbits
and stored them in the attic. Now
ev-ry-thing has its place. Then nothing.

No more pencils scratching off lists
nor rhythm and beat of projects
to fill my days. After all this

I drive my wagon team emptied
of chores and obligations
to the overlook of an unscheduled life

with its broad and frightening plain.

A Gift to Myself
~upon occasion of my sixty-fifth year

Goodbye to self-doubt and second guessing
—the what ifs and should haves. Gone
are decisions of little consequence, anything

that needs ironing! I give myself permission
to ask for help—the sooner the better—
and drop books that don't hold my attention.

I keep in my purse a souvenir button:
I may be compelled to face danger,
but not fear it, from the home of Clara Barton.

Portrait of a Husband

Ask him, What color are
her eyes? He'll say, Two.
Or, What kind of tree is that?

He'll say, Green. Or what type
of shoes the children are wearing,
he'll say, One for each foot.

But ask him the best play of the '55 World Series,
he'll say, late in the Seventh game, Yogi Berra's
hard drive to left corner caught by Sandy Amaros.

Or ask him the best shot in golf history? He'll say,
2005 Masters, 16th hole, Tiger pitches from the fringe.
His ball made a hard right to the top of the green

to trickle in for a birdie. And ask him where I left
my glasses, how I brush my hair, what disarms me,
he'll say, I notice what is important.

Fallen Pine

It is immense
my arms cannot circle it.
Last night's downburst snapped
its base like a bone. I pose, a weight-lifter,
beneath the trunk, hear pine-bore beetles
grind the pulp.

We step off its hundred feet
feel the slow fall of time
from its hundred years.

Will we have the privilege
of a long life?

I don't know but if you fall
       I will catch you.

Epilogue

Dear Ann,

We share the distinction of being selected as poets in Muddy Ford Press's laureate series. Most moments of joy are inexplicably brief but thankfully recalled in birdsong and sunrise, poetry and song, and kindnesses. Hold onto joy's temporariness for as long as you can. There is the generous joy of Cindi Boiter's and Bob Jolley's advocation to publish and celebrate voices. There is the lasting joy of Ed Madden's editorial care and poetic guidance, as well as the courage of final choices.

Soon, strangers will whisper they've connected to your poems like a lost twin. There will be moments of sacred exchange with other poets with gusts of joyous air. Your face will light with the pride of friends and family that have shared your journey and companionable silences. Before each reading, whisper a prayer to the pain of failed attempts and the work of verse. Never forget your effort to search for words and rhythms to reveal your meaning.

Let these pages open you up to joy more than ever before in this thin papery life to absorb every ounce of the life-work within your collection. Recall each instant when these lines first kissed your lips and sparked breath alive. Your poems won't ever forget you. When your book finds niches on shelves, and stanzas are voiced across kitchen islands, you'll know the astonishment of being known more deeply than before. There is mending when a poet discovers what must be written, and already within you is the stirring of next collections. Together in our shared bond with Cindi, Bob, and Ed, we must encourage and help others find their voices, so they, too, know the astonishing joy of being heard.

With praise and great love,
Tim Conroy
March 4, 2020

Acknowledgements

Grateful acknowledgment is made to the editors of the following journals and projects in which some of these poems first appeared, sometimes in slightly different form:

Fall Lines, "Baptism" and "A Doe in Repose"; *Jasper Magazine*, "Columbia's Irish Canal Digger" and "Camp Sorghum"; *Syzygy*, "An Eclipse and a Butcher"; *The Collective I*, "Fine with Blind"; Poetry Society of South Carolina, "Three Dreams"; Poems on the Bus, "The Virtual Tour" and "Catch-light".

I am especially grateful to Bob Jolley and Cindi Boiter, publishers, and Ed Madden, editor and Columbia's Poet Laureate, for the Laureate Series published through Muddy Ford Press in which this book appears. Thanks also to the incomparable Tim Conroy and to Christina Xan, who provided invaluable assistance in revising and editing this manuscript—I could not have completed this work as easily and efficiently without her kind and careful assistance.

My poems have been deeply influenced by participation in the City of Columbia's Poet Laureate initiatives and public arts projects, such as Poems on the Comet, as well as by my participation in the Writing in Place workshops offered by Hub City Press. My work has also been influenced by Allen University's series on religion and art; the South Carolina Book Festival and Deckle Edge Literary Festival; the Bones of the Spirit reading series organized by Al Black; and the many opportunities made possible through the Poetry Society of South Carolina.

I am grateful to South Carolina's Poet Laureate, Marjory Wentworth and Columbia Museum of Art's Poet-in-Residence and Chair of the SC Academy of Authors, Ray McManus.

Special recognition for the institutional treasures that are such a part of my work: Richland Library (Main Branch and Sandhills), South Carolina State Library, Talking Books Library, Columbia Museum of Art, the University of South Carolina's Office of Disabilities, and the Thomas Cooper Library at USC. I am also grateful to the talented and generous USC poetry professors Nikky Finney, Tara Powell, and Fred Dings; to English Department Chair, Nina Levine; and to Mary Baskin Waters and Brian Glavey. Thanks as well to Wheaton College English professors Richard and Alison Caviness Gibson; to Krista Bremer of *The Sun Magazine*; and to the poets Kwame Dawes, Jessica Jacobs, and Nickole Brown.

Special thanks to wise and talented poets and close readers: Susan Craig, Betsy Thorne, Delia Corrigan, Libby Bernardin, and graduate students Arianna Miller, Melanie E. Walker, Annie Kolle, and Lindsey Kim. Thanks also to the USC Writing Center directors: Deidre Garriott and Christopher Holcomb.

Thanks to the Shepherd's Center for community writing classes and The FriendShip.org for the generosity of their volunteers.

I am grateful for the professional skills and friendships of Leah Lake, Anika Ali, Adelaide Kline, Hope Spillane, Billie Muthig, Dawn Helps, Bradley Crain, Dow Hammond, Amanda Noyes, Curtis Derrick, Linda Murphey, Margot Robinson, Rosalie Ramm, Debbie Bouche, Donna McGreevy, Sally Mullen, Donna Lais, Trish Sargent, Molly and Will Sherman, Francie Markham, Mary Rushing Jones, Linda Marie Kirkpatrick, Rebecca McMenemy, poetry classmates, book club companions, PSSC poets, and musicians Lance Roper and Bill Johns.

I am especially appreciative to the Taylor family: Mary Taylor, and her late husband Dr. Edmund Taylor, their daughter, Mary Beverley, and her husband, Imtiaz Haque.

Special thanks to nature photographers, Kathryn Newsom, Sparkle Clark, and Marian Davis for introducing me to buttermilk skies, the Blue Hour, and birdsong.

I could not have completed this project without the help of Apple Accessibility Support; my magnificent guide dogs, Brego and Monty; and the Southeastern Guide Dog family, especially Karen Gruver, Karen Newsome, Patricia Allen, and Thomas O'Shea.

I am incredibly grateful to Michael Nye, author of *My Heart Is Not Blind*, for eloquent profiles of those of us who see with more than our eyes, and his wife and poet, Naomi Shihab Nye.

Many thanks to my Spring Valley Presbyterian Church family; my niece Eleanor Baker for website design; Baker and Susan Craig for cover design; family in-laws Grover, Treva, and Jack; sons, Brad and Charlie, and their families; and husband since 1979, Kirk.

And special thanks to the exceptional Sarah Ashworth and the Ashworth family.

About the Poet

Ann-Chadwell Humphries lives in Columbia, SC. As a girl, Ann competed in school poetry recitation through the University Interscholastic League in Leakey and Austin, Texas. Ann took Honors English in college, yet only after retirement did Ann begin to write poetry through community writing classes. She has also taken graduate poetry classes at the University of South Carolina, poetry workshops at Wofford College, and online classes through University of Iowa, University of Pennsylvania, and the Hadley Institute for the Blind.

Her work has appeared in *Jasper*, *Emrys*, *The Collective I*, Indolent Books' What Rough Beast series, and the Poems on the Comet series, a public poetry project that puts writing on city buses. She was the winner of a *Sun Magazine* scholarship, recipient of an Emerging Voices award through the Jasper Project, and a winner in the Poetry Society of South Carolina's annual contests. She reads and writes her work using assistive technology.

www.ingramcontent.com/pod-product-compliance
Lightning Source LLC
Chambersburg PA
CBHW052122110526
44592CB00013B/1710